E

For Dogs:

Dog Care Safe Natural Aromatherapy Remedies, Recipes For Canines, Puppies, Pets

By

Angela Pierce

Table of Contents

Introduction 5

Chapter 1. Essential Oils Basics 7

Chapter 2. Risks 12

Chapter 3. Benefits and Practical Uses 16

    Calm 16

    Skin and Coat 19

    Doggy Breath 23

    Additional Tips 25

Chapter 4. Additional Recipes 27

Final Words 30

Thank You Page 32

Essential Oils For Dogs: Dog Care Safe Natural
Aromatherapy Remedies, Recipes For Canines,
Puppies, Pets

By Angela Pierce

First Published, 2015

Printed in the United States of America

Introduction

At this point, you've already heard of essential oils. The pure, distilled, mega-factor of a plant's life. They're comprised of powerful chemicals that can aid and assist your body (or your dog's body) to perform to their fullest capacity. By utilizing this natural medicine, you can encourage both health and healing. In fact, most of our 'modern' medicines are derived from natural sources, and by getting straight to the point, you can not only cut costs (financially), but also cut down on negative side effects associated with our over-strong synthesized veterinary medications.

You and your believed canine can actually share in the health benefits delivered by most of these natural remedies, and they can be used to treat anything from nervousness and hyperactivity, to hypertension, digestive disorders, and liver trouble, to healthy skin and hair (who wouldn't want that...be it dog or human compatriot). Learning about and using essential oils can absolutely change the way you view health.

Sharing your knowledge of natural botanical extracts is a kindness few dog owners get to proffer, and in doing so, you ensure a healthier, happier life for your canine friend. These are nature's own true remedies, and your dog is you own true companion...it's a natural fit and one that will bring you both happiness and health for years to come. But, don't underestimate how powerful these remedies can be. Concentrated plant extracts can help treat malignancies, organ disorders and mental/nervous conditions, just as they can cause tremendous harm, neuropathy, and even death. Read on to give yourself a simple foundational knowledge regarding the world of plant extracts, yourself, and your dog.

Chapter 1. Essential Oils Basics

What actually is an essential oil (you ask)? Well, the concept is interesting, and ages old in its development. So, let's begin with what we know for sure –life requires water. That being the case, life also requires a means to isolate, sequester, store, transport, and accumulate water…here-in lies you answer. Every living thing (even sea creatures) have the need to create compounds that are "hydrophobic". Hydro – water…Phobic – fearing (think of someone with a "phobia"). These are necessary compounds, and all living things possess them (you and I as well). Some of these hydrophobic compounds come in the form of waxes (African violet and mimosa) and others in the form of oils. These oils take crafty resourcefulness to create.

In nature, oils are fairly complex compounds. Far more complex than most sugars, or lignans, or even most starches. They require multiple ingredients that must be drawn from the earth. As such, plants (far older than we humans) have found myriad ways to construct oils and waxes out of what they've had available to them.

What is an essential oil?

An essential oil is the material extracted from a plant that does not contain any water. They are the complex chemical compounds created by a plant in order to help it survive and reproduce. The compounds in essential oils may contain extremely complex molecules, substances yet unsynthesized in a laboratory. Furthermore, there is an array of compounds in any one natural essential oil. Often times, it is the synergistic effect of two or more compounds working in harmony that gives us the desired health benefit. Many essential oils have not been fully documented, so at this time, we cannot know exactly why certain oils have certain health benefits. What we can know, through decades of modern testing as well as centuries of homeopathic systems worldwide, is that essential oils are a powerful tool in your medicine bag. They are not toys, they are far more than a pretty smell, and if not treated with respect and deference, they can have serious damaging effects.

Essential oils can be made from nearly every part of the plant: Flowers, leaves, stems, bark, roots, rhizomes, seeds (nuts), or berries, fruits, pods, etc. Some parts of the plant contain only trace amounts of extremely potent oils, and these cannot be extracted through a simple mechanical process like described above. Instead, these oils are collected through some form of distillation. Gathering of these oils is a very labor intensive process, and the ultimate yields are extremely low. These oils are called 'absolute' (as in Chamomile Flower Absolute Essential Oil).

Essential oils refer to the oils recovered from some living thing (most typically plants). Some plants produce a high volume of oil (think about olives) and others, far less (cinnamon). Lavender oil, for instance, requires about one-hundred pounds of raw plant material to produce 1 pound of mid-quality oil; good quality rose oil requires 8,000lbs. to make one pound of oil. The plant (or material) is typically heated or centrifuged to remove some excess water, and then pressed to extract the oils. The oils are then treated to remove additional water (water will destabilize the product as well as shorten its shelf life).

It is very important to use only the highest quality oils, without additives or any foreign agents. This is to ensure that you know exactly what you're putting into your body (or onto and in your dog's body). Never purchase or use any agent of which you are not completely certain.

Picking an essential oil

When shopping for oils to establish or add to your collection, purity and quality are what you need. First let's talk about purity. How pure is pure enough? Typically you want to go with 100% if you can afford it. This way you know exactly what you are using, you know there is no possibility of a contraindication due to an additive ingredient, and you get be certain of your dosages when mixing different oils to perform a certain function. The label on the bottle should read "100% Pure xxx Oil. If you have to go with an option less than 100% purity, then the ingredients should be on the label. Often times, essential oils will be mixed with jojoba oil, olive or safflower oil, or some other adjutant oil. As long as you are familiar with these products, they can still be highly effective. Generally when an oil comes at less than 100% strength, it is a highly potent essential. In fact, many plant oils are harmful or even dangerous in their pure state. As long as you are using a reputable product, these adulterated oils can be absolutely fine.

Chapter 2. Risks

Like we've said, essential oils are powerful. This means they have the same power to perform good as they have the power to do harm. Used responsibly, EO can be beneficial tools. There are many EOs that are beneficial to humans which can be devastating to your canine friend. Though many oils are of common use for humans, the bodies of dogs may process them differently, or in the case of some, not process them at all. This can result in toxic organ failure, tachycardia, depressed nervous function, slowed breathing, and even death. For some of these oils, the plant itself is not toxic at all (basil is good for your dog if your dog likes it) but the extremely concentrated oil can be fatal (basil oil contains potentially hazardous phenylpropanoids).

Because this industry is fairly new, and because EO are not regulated by any official body, high-quality scientific testing results are slow in developing. Much evidence is anecdotal, and frequently there seem to be mitigating factors involved when someone tells their tale of woe regarding essential oils and the death of a beloved pet (the pet was very old, infirmed, pregnant, or the application of the oil was administered incorrectly or with accident). Again, your best option is to get in touch with a local veterinarian (if yours doesn't already administer EO at their office) and also to educate yourself regarding the various potential interactions between animals and EOs. A short list of some essential oils most likely to be hazardous to your dog would have to include: Anything containing Phenols (thyme, oregano), Pine derivatives, wormwood, garlic (good as a whole ingredient, too strong as an oil), bitter almond, camphor, mugwort, wintergreen, and clove oil (again, far too strong). In general, even when utilizing the safest of oils (parsley, liver oil, copaiba), they should be diluted and administered in a way to prevent any possibility of overdose.

The two EO that get the most attention when it comes to treating animals are Tea-Tree Oil, and Pennyroyal. This is probably because they are so common on the market. Tea-tree is huge for human consumption. It's used to treat minor skin abrasions and dryness, to aid digestion, or improves one's breath. We humans can use tea-tree at full strength in any application we choose, and worst case scenario, we risk a mild burning sensation, or slight discomfort. This is not true for your pet. 100% concentrate tea-tree is far too strong even for a large dog. This isn't so much about body mass index, as it is about the skin of animals processing foreign substances differently than we do. The other toxin that is (incredibly) common is actually added to pet products ON PURPOSE, and by the PET COMPANY! It is an ingredient found commonly in flea and tick preventatives and it is called Pennyroyal. Now, this botanical has been proven highly effective in discouraging fleas and ticks. The only downside is that it does appear to have a cumulative effect on your pet's system. It appears that your pet has no way to process some of the metabolites created after pennyroyal is absorbed through the animal's skin.

In every case (yup, EVERY case) it is safer and more effective to administer the essential oils in a slower mode over a longer time period until the desired result is achieved, rather than trying for a one-dose success. This is because even within species, or year to year within the same individual animal, tolerances, organ function, skin conditions, etc. fluctuate and vary. Also consider this: no two bottles of essential oil are alike (unless they have the same lot and batch number, then they are basically the same). So caution must always be exercised when using a new bottle, and especially a new brand.

Probably the best expectation you can hope for is to establish a healthy regimen for your dog, and then maintain that health through regular doses of the EOs you choose to apply. Essential oils are good to treat acute external conditions, but when it comes to internal conditions ,it's better to take it slow and hope to promote health through consistency.

Chapter 3. Benefits and Practical Uses

Now that we have established the risks involved with EO and dogs, and we understand what it takes to make safe informed purchases of high quality oils for use on you and your pooch (that's one nice benefit...no need for separate medicine chests) let's talk briefly about the benefits of using essential oils. Briefly, because we could spend days discussing the possibilities of improving and prolonging the life of the dog you love.

Calm

Most animals will respond to calming agents placed in the proximity of their environment. This can be extremely beneficial for you and the animal both, when traveling, entertaining company, or paying a visit to the vet. Remember though, your dog is far more sensitive than you. Some dogs can actually become overwhelmed by any powerful smell. In some cases, even a calming agent can actually cause stress to your dog. As always, when applying EO for your dog, watch for any signs of distress. These can include panting, vocalizations, dulled reflexes, or anything out of the ordinary. To administer a calming agent, maybe begin with lavender. It's frequently successful, well tolerated, and rarely leads to unwanted reactions.

First diffuse the oil (lavender or bergamot work well) in some other agent (like olive oil). Then drip a bit of the diluted oil onto sawdust, or pencil shavings, or small animal bedding. Wrap that in a porous cloth (like cheesecloth) and hang like a sachet somewhere adjacent to (NOT WITHIN) your animals environment. Large animals, like your dog, that have the ability to avoid something they don't like can be introduced directly to the sachet and be left to decide for themselves if they want to breathe that or not. Always watch for signs of discomfort, distress, or labored breathing, and remove the animal to fresh air at once if any negative change occurs.

Another way to administer calming agents is through a hydrolysis diffuser. This is a simple and inexpensive machine that sends a mist into the environment, bathing an area of your home in the EO you have chosen. This is nice because you get to enjoy the product as well. What's good for your dog is *usually* good for you as well (though the opposite is certainly not true).

Skin and Coat

Your dog naturally produces oils that keep its skin healthy and its coat shiny and sleek. Because we want to spend time with and near our dogs, we like to keep them clean. Far cleaner than they could ever be in the wild, or even as an outdoor dogs. The downside of this is that it does disrupt their natural oil productions.

This can eventually lead to dry skin, itchiness, flaky skin, and even more serious conditions that can range from unpleasant and uncomfortable, to serious conditions or even infections that can require hospitalization.

By utilizing EO for your dog, you can make up for much of the damage that washing and shampoo inflicts on your dog's skin. You can mix the oils you wish to administer into olive oil, or coconut oil. There was a great study done that shows that EO treatment was as effective as the traditional treatment of chemical application. Malassezia is a type of yeast that typically lives on the skin of dogs, but can, at times, grow out of control, inhabit the dog's skin, and causing itching and discomfort.

Recipes

For your dog's skin and coat consider these blends:

Healthy Sheen – 2 parts Bitter Orange, 1 part Myrtle, 1 part Rose oil, blend in jojoba

Dry Skin/eczema – 1 part Yarrow, 1 part Spearmint, 1 part Rosemary, 1part Cypress

Cuts and Scrapes – 1 part Lemon balm, 1 part Rose oil, 1 part sassafras dilute in coconut or olive oil 10:1
This can be applied directly to the chafed or abraded area. Leave uncovered until oils are absorbed into the skin (min. 30 minutes) If the wound is in an area accessible to your dog, the application of the oil may induce licking. This is fine. Be careful if you decide to reapply, as overconsumption of the oils can lead to stomach distress.

All Natural Sunscreen: This one works as well on your skin as it does on your dog's sensitive parts.

Different oils have differing SPF ratings. Here is a short list with the approximated ratings:

Almond Oil has SPF 5, Zinc Oxide has SPF 2-20, Coconut Oil- SPF 4-6, Seed Oil Red Raspberry has SPF 25-50, Shea Butter – SPF 4-6, Carrot Seed Oil has SPF 35-40.

To create your sunscreen, you'll need a pan of boiling water and a mason jar. Add some beeswax, or shea butter, or hydrolyzed coconut wax into the mason jar and wait for it to melt. Add your oils, a few drops at a time, until you reach the desired (approximate) SPF rating; usually go for SPF20-40. If you choose, you can add zinc oxide to increase effectiveness, however you may choose to omit this ingredient if you have concerns regarding ingestion.

Mix the ingredients in the jar and allow to cool slowly. It should result in a thick liquid once cooled, which you can apply just like over-the-counter sunscreens. Enjoy!

Some other oils that are safe and effective for dogs coats include: Copaiba (Copaiba officinalis), Helichrysum (H. italicum), Peppermint (Mentha piperita), as well as all the normal digestive oils like those of parsley, lemongrass, wheatgrass, barley, and Chrysanthemum.

Peppermint oils, heavily diluted, are wonderful to add a healthy sheen to your dog's coat. And copaiba is wonderful as a skin bracer, and shows signs of being a power anti-inflammatory (especially in older dogs).

When administering EO to your dog's coat and skin, the application couldn't be any simpler. Simply mix your solution and if you want, cut it with olive oil, coconut oil, or jojoba (which is becoming very popular). Then simply stroke the oil into the hair and coat of your dog. This can be a pleasant bonding experience, which is not always the case with a trip to the vet. As always, when applying essential oils (on dogs or people) watch for any signs of change. There is always the potential for your dog to develop a sensitivity, and this can happen at any time. Watch for licking or scratching in excess or in unusual areas. This may indicate discomfort due to the application of the oils. If you suspect that something is wrong, discontinue use and consult your veterinarian.

Doggy Breath

It's not the dog's fault, it's natural. What many people don't realize is that most doggy breath issues actually start in the stomach. Brushing your dog's teeth won't solve the problem. What you need to do is treat the problem at the source.

One simple solution is a bit of parsley oil in your dog's dish. It's simple and effective and has the added bonus of settling your dog's stomach in general. Now, not all dogs will readily eat their food with an EO added to it. We all know how finicky dogs can be. The solution to this problem is simple as well.

Begin with almost no oil at all. Half a drop in a dish of food is the place to start. Hopefully your dog doesn't mind that tiny amount. Then each day, or even every few days (if your dog is very picky) up the dose by another half a drop. Continue to increase the dose daily or every several days until you eventually reach the desired dose. You dog will most likely come to appreciate the oil in their food, as they begin to associate it with feeling better. After you reach this point, it is more likely you'll be able to add other oils without protest.

Recipes

Sweet Breath- 2 parts Anise, 1 part Bergamot, 1 part Lemongrass

Teeth and Gums- 1 part Oregano, 1 part Black Pepper, 1 part Parsley

Indigestion- 1 part Patchouli, 1 part Tarragon, 1 part Juniper, 1 part Ginger, 1 part Fennel

This solution will treat your dog's nervous stomach conditions, but can also be used to soothe during car rides and other travel. Even for dogs that get nervous in new surroundings, this will help to calm and settle their stomachs. What some dog owners do it to always use the same mixture of oils, and essentially have a "nervous time" food. This way, your dog comes to a positive association with stressful periods, and will come to appreciate the benefits of their 'special food'.

Additional Tips

Now, unlike many other animals that are the source of terrifying stories regarding the misuse of essential oils, dogs tend to be far more robust. Oils can be applied to their coat, but it is often essential that at least some of the compound be taken orally. For this reason, it is often necessary for dogs, that you put a few DILUTED drops of the EO mixed directly into their food. Some dogs can be particularly finicky about what they eat and this can cause a problem. For those dogs that won't eat food with a strange additive, try introducing the oil directly to the dog in the form of a dilute solution and a dropper. Or, perhaps mix the oil into a favorite treat (like peanut butter). One more method is to slowly increase the amount of oil you add to your dogs food. Begin with ½ a drop and then add one-half more each day until you are up to dose. In this manner, should should build a gradual acceptance in your dog to the new sensation. This is also a good way to introduce your dog to EO without the risk of digestive distress in dogs with a sensitive stomach.

Proper oils can aid in digestion, promote healthier skin and coat, improve natural defenses against infection, and help to dissuade fleas, ticks, and other parasites from choosing your pup as their new home. Some oils that are safe and effective for dogs include: the Fennel(Foeniculum vulgare), Copaiba (Copaifera officinalis), Oregano (Origanum vulgare), Thyme (Thymus vulgaris), Lavender (Lavandula angustifolia), Basil (Ocimum basilicum), Marjoram (Origanum majorana), Cypress (Cupressus sempervirens), Peppermint (Mentha piperita), Catnip (Nepeta cataria), and lastly the Frankincense (Boswellia carterii).

Chapter 4. Additional Recipes

Calm- 1 part Peppermint, 1 part Myrrh, 1 part Violet Leaf Extract

Energizer- 1 part Thyme, 1 part Rosemary, 1 part Ginger, 1 part Grapefruit

Graceful Aging- 1 part Grapefruit, 1 part Hyssop, 1 part Coriander, 1 part Roman Chamomile

Joint Health- 2 parts Juniper, 1 part wintergreen, 1 part Orange Blossom, 1 part Elder Flower
This mixture is best diluted into your aging dog's water dish. A few drops per day will suffice to help your dog maintain joint health into its golden years.

Insect Repellent – 2 parts Citronella, 1 part Eucalyptus, 1 part Cedar, 1 part Sandalwood
Apply frequently and liberally. Brush deep into the coat to promote absorption into the skin.

Ear Care- 1 part Rosemary, 1 part Cedar, 1 part Lemon, 1 part Hyssop

This is ideal for soothing the effects of ear mites and other ear discomfort, and may prevent additional infestation

Dry Nose- 1 part Chamomile, 1 part Oleander, dilute 10:1 in olive oil
Your dog's nose is so sensitive. If it dries out (often the case in older dogs) it can become uncomfortable to them. Use this solution sparingly in order to ensure that you dog stays at peak health.

Paws- 3 parts Bitter Orange, 1 part Lemongrass, 1 part Ginger, 1 part Sweet Almond   -mix in coconut or jojoba
This recipe can be applied liberally at any time. Not only will the ingredients soothe cracked and dry paws and pads, but once absorbed they will put an energetic spring in your dog's step.

Weight Loss- 1 part Grapefruit, 1 part Rapeseed, 1 part Lemon, 1part Bergamot, 1 part Jasmine,1 part Honeysuckle
This mixture can be added to your dog's water, or to their food. The flavor is rather strong, so some dog's might reject it at first. This mixture even helps when

absorbed through the skin, so if there's no way to get your dog to take it orally, that is another alternative.

Final Words

Start slowly with the simplest and safest of oils, and slowly build your collection as your knowledge grows. Take hysterical hype with a grain of salt, whether it be for or against EO; it is too rich a subject to distill into one anecdote or another. Ultimately, your pet's health and well being are in your hands.

The only concern you need have is that you might overdo it. Botanicals, and essential oils, especially, can be an incredible contribution to the health of both you and your pets. Take the time to learn about the potential risks and rewards for the animals you love. Speak with your vet, but if they do not practice with EO themselves, then consult a veterinarian who does.

Many vets are beginning to explore the potentials of essential oils, both in their own lives and in their practice. There is not the same sense of resistance often found in human medicine to alternative treatments. Anyone familiar with farm life knows how these tools have been used everyday with cows, horses, sheep, etc. Clearly we know that essential oils work.

It is an exciting time we live in, full of research and breakthroughs almost daily. There is a resurgence in the interest of ages-old wisdom, and in combining modern technology with the time tested compounds nature provides, we will lead healthier happier lives. The same can be true for your pet...don't you owe it to them to learn more?

Thank You Page

I want to personally thank you for reading my book. I hope you found information in this book useful and I would be very grateful if you could leave your honest review about this book. I certainly want to thank you in advance for doing this.

If you have the time, you can check my other books too.

CPSIA information can be obtained
at www.ICGtesting.com
Printed in the USA
LVOW05s0759260517

535915LV00023B/451/P

9 781681 858784